HOW TO
SPOT A
HIPSTER

HOW TO
SPOT A
HIPSTER

BY
JEREMY
CASSAR

ILLUSTRATIONS
BY CARLA McRAE

Smith
Street
Books

C/23_ 🔲 PACKED METRO BE LIKE ✌

TABLE OF CONTENTS

INTRODUCTION

At some point between the years 2016 and the hour before our universe collapses into itself, man will comb the timelines of history and pay respects to the human movements that fought to correct its course – the revolutionaries, the Romantics, the crusaders, the inventors … the hipsters.

What is a hipster? *NB: Not to be confused with 1940's hipsters, who were cool, but nowhere near as cool as the modern version.*

Early in the 21st century, this carefully constructed collage of a subculture wrapped the Western world in a gigantic pair of skinny-legged jeans and maintained the tightest of grips, while its members banded together to blend disparate styles and forms into some mutating haze of aesthetic energy. (If you were to fold a cardboard hipster into multiple sections, you might think each derives from a different individual.)

In other words, just as jesters are full of jest and boasters are full of boast, hipsters are full of… well, whatever's hip at that specific junction in time, as long as the masses have never heard of it.

For such a pervasive sub-come-mainstream culture, it's not always easy to tell the difference between a hipster and a human. Laypeople are known to scratch their heads and furrow their brows at passing youths, dizzy with indecision.

Early on in the movement, one could spot a hipster relatively easily. Clearly identifiable criteria existed – a guy who wouldn't ordinarily have a beard, had a beard, or a girl wore thick-rimmed glasses and a pixie haircut. Since then, identification has become much more complicated. Hipster sects have popped up in every corner of every urban city, each one fenced within a specific – yet oddly elusive – set of parameters.

How to Spot a Hipster attempts to break down the hipster phenomenon into (hand-harvested, organic) digestible chunks. Fixie-bike riding through all stations of the subculture including fashion, grooming and lifestyle, this comprehensive manual will ensure that you never again appear foolish in front of someone you don't understand by misusing the h-word, and will prove a handy tool for revealing if, in fact, you yourself are a hipster.

Literally.

FIELD GUIDE

An illustrated overview of different hipster types:

THE ART HIPSTER

Identifying features: bowl haircut; shapeless clothing with textiles designed by local artists

* Natural habitat: small gallery openings
* Diet: anything from a food truck, and free cask wine

✦✦✦✦✦✦✦

THE MOUNTAIN MAN

Identifying features: full, luscious beard; tartan flannel shirt; unused artisanal hand-axe

* Natural habitat: inner-city neighbourhoods where wilderness is an unruly balcony garden
* Diet: kimchi tacos, sriracha waffles and ramen

The Mountain Man   The Art Hipster

The Music
Festival Waif

THE MUSIC FESTIVAL WAIF

Identifying features: some sort of culturally-appropriated headgear (Native American headdress, Indian hair chains and bindis), combat boots, metallic tattoos, crochet bikini top

- Natural habitat: the festival so indie that only 156 tickets are available each year
- Diet: falafel from the Hare Krishna tent

❖❖❖❖❖❖❖

THE MIXOLOGIST

Identifying features: shirt sleeves carefully rolled to artfully display tats, waxed moustache, bowtie, braces

- Natural habitat: behind the bars of reservation-only prohibition-era speakeasies with hidden entrances
- Diet: artisanal bitters, small-batch gin, hand chiselled ice spheres and maraschino cherries

The Mixologist

The Tech 'Creative'

THE TECH 'CREATIVE'

Identifying features: Macbook Air, SXSW hoodie, DSLR

* **Natural habitat:** found 'killing it' at warehouse conversion co-working spaces surrounded by other creative entrepreneurs who are also 'killing it'
* **Diet:** free pizza and sponsored craft beer from networking events and 'meet-ups'

◆◆◆◆◆◆◆◆

THE ETSY ENTREPRENEUR

Identifying features: bangs, big glasses, handmade flower crown, vintage floral dress, owl necklace

* **Natural habitat:** thrift stores and flea markets, sourcing materials for their next jewellery range inspired by woodland creatures
* **Diet:** raw vegan cupcakes, ice tea

The Etsy Entrepreneur

The Barista

The Tortured Poet

THE BARISTA

Identifying features: beanie, leather apron, incredulous sneer when asked to make a soy cappuccino

- **Natural habitat:** ex-motorcycle garages converted into coffee roasters
- **Diet:** cold-drip iced pour-over made from beans air-lifted directly from the side of a volcano in Guatamala

✦✦✦✦✦✦✦

THE TORTURED POET

Identifying features: black skinny jeans, white v-neck t-shirt, keffiyeh, battered copy of *On the Road* or *Naked Lunch*

- **Natural habitat:** in the darkest corner of the local cafe
- **Diet:** whatever's left at the local soup kitchen after the actual homeless people have been fed

PHYSICAL ATTRIBUTES

Overalls

Nana cardigan

Plaid shirt

V-neck tee

Skinny jeans

KEY FASHION PIECES

Like cookies are to Girl Guides, no human can begin their ascent up the hipster ladder without a few staple possessions. This subculture starter-pack includes:

Skinny jeans — Since the dawn of the modern hipster, skinny jeans have acted as a cultural touchstone. The medical community is yet to comment on whether future generations will suffer from low-blood circulation in the legs and reproductive abnormalities, as hipsters have also infiltrated the medical community. Getting in and out of this item of clothing is a challenge that requires preparation and practice, which has indirectly led to a considerable drop in impulsive sexual relations and therefore, a drop in unwanted pregnancy and the transmission of STI's.

Plaid shirt buttoned up to the neck — Formerly a fashion choice reserved for Latin American street gangs, hipsters decided that style was far more important than the ability to breathe without constriction. When worn with a hefty beard, this look gives the illusion of a neck-less hipster.

Knitwear — Tight wool-wear was once synonymous with bespectacled men who spent a tad too much time reading newspapers near local school playgrounds, but these days, every hipster's wardrobe contains one or more suffocating sweaters. Bonus points if rendered in khaki, burgundy, beige or mustard. Conversely, a hipster can go for the looser, more familial garment – the oversized nana cardigan.

Dungarees or bib-and-brace overalls — It makes no difference whether a hipster has done a hard day's labour on a farm or not, one-piece denim workwear is no longer associated with hillbillies and hicks.

V-neck tee — A tee-cut that was largely worn by British boy bands and Dexter the serial killer now hugs the torsos of hipsters worldwide. The V of this tee doubles as a practical spot for hipsters to hang their Ray-Ban Wayfarers.

FOOTWEAR

It is a common recommendation that humans never go the cheap route when it comes to feet, as sub-par footwear can lead to a long list of unnecessarily physical issues later in life. The hipster community knows this is merely Big Shoe propaganda, and that in every case, style trumps the ability to walk in a consistent direction.

Combat boots — Girl hipsters can commonly be spotted wearing sizeable old boots with brown socks, paired with the skimpiest vintage floral dress available. This is a look that says "I'm legit girly yet ready to, like, literally jump boots-first into Manic-Pixie-Dream-Girl adventures."

Sneakers with everything — When unsure of what to do with their feet, hipsters generally opt for a pair of classic sneakers – preferably Nikes. This footwear staple can be worn with any outfit – from suits to sweats to swimwear.

Keds or other sandshoes — Keds are the original sneaker and are loved by hipsters as they tend to flock to 'original' anything. As more and more pick up on the Keds trend, hipsters have refined the scope of this choice to vintage Keds from the 60s or in ideal cases, a tattered pair of the original Keds from 1916.

Brogues — A versatile shoe used in various hipster ensembles, brogues gives the walker an op-shop look while retaining the ability to boast about a designer price tag. They add a sleekness to the already skinny-legged jean, and are a vital component in achieving the 'nana' look.

Shoes without socks — It is rumoured that hipsters fetishise bare ankles. Convincing evidence backs this rumour, as socks are no longer a necessary component of a hipster's day-to-day outfit. Though the less genuine hipster will consider the atmosphere in their immediate area and sheathe their feet in a discreet pair of sockettes, authentic hipsters go commando.

Sneakers

Combat boots

Sandshoes

Brogues

Tattoo

Another tattoo

"Like, so many tattoos, hey?"

TATTOOS

Marking one's body with a combination of permanent ink and shallow scarring is no longer synonymous with those who eye-gouge barflies and cook meth. In fact, criminals have migrated from the tattoo-parlour scene due to a mysterious and in-no-way coincidental case of collective nausea. Society must concede that hipsters – from the nerd-chic to the convincingly rockabilly – have divided-and-conquered the ink world.

Sleeve tattoos — Like the beard, sleeve tattoos ratchet up the hipster's attractiveness level to the power of ten, whether or not one's arm is toned or plump.

Neck and finger tattoos — At this moment, legions of murderers and gangsters, both incarcerated and on the outside, are fashioning shivs for the purpose of either amputating their finger or removing a wedge of neck flesh. Hipsters have now claimed these once-rebellious markings, and unfortunately there's not a single tattoo-removal clinic in the clink.

Geometric tattoos — An unfilled filled geometric shape on hipster skin reflects their devotion to sophisticated, minimalist design – a fixed-gear bicycle in ink form. The hipster often explains their tattoo as based on an obscure mathematical theorem (which they've memorised just in case they're asked about it).

Nostalgia tattoos — Hipsters are known to select a pop-cultural obsession from their youth and incorporate it into their permanent presentation: Care Bears, My Little Pony, Astroboy, Voltron – basically anything you'd find in a Tokyo trinket mall.

Hipster tattoo bingo — When you're out hipster-watching, why not play a spot of hipster tattoo bingo? Key tattoos to add to your card are: tree, branch, constellation, arrow, triangle, feather, bird, deer, wolf, pineapple, vintage camera, dreamcatcher, anchor, owl, fox.

PRINTED TEES AND JUMPERS

Wearing your heart on your sleeveless tee or skin-tight sweater is the direct opposite of hipster, but brandishing an obscure, quirky print can be a great way to draw the eye – much like the feature wall in a Williamsburg or Shoreditch loft apartment. The following stylistic choices are not only fashionable but also a cheeky nod to the hipster's ironic sensibilities:

Intentionally-tacky illustrations of wild animals in their natural habitats — The busier the drawing, and the more of the garment's surface area it encompasses, the better. These can be matched with a like-printed set of bargain basement pillowslips.

Retro gaming — The more obscure the better. For example, a promotional t-shirt for Journey, the 1983 arcade game inspired by the stadium-rock band of the same name. These garments can be well worn and authentic, or boutique reproductions.

Second-hand tees from business conferences or expos from before you were born — For example, an official 1987 Lombard Insurance Management Conference t-shirt, complete with remnants of an old name tag. This stylistic choice is also likely to represent clever commentary on the redundancy of corporate culture.

Second-hand
tees from
business
conferences

Retro gaming insignia

Intentionally tacky
illustrations of
wild animals

Moleskine

Macbook

Keffiyeh

Leather bag

Trucker cap

Large headphones

ACCESSORIES

If a prominent toy company were to sell a hipster action figurine, they could easily suck consumers dry with an unending range of separately sold accessories. Here is a tiny sample of what you might find on a hipster's person:

Leather bag and Macbook — A must have for any hipster sitting solo at a café – this accessory combo impresses with its weathered charms and suggestions of intellect. The savvy hipster will ensure their Macbook is open to a running Word document at all times, to disguise the fact that they're just browsing Tumblr and Imgur.

Moleskine journal — The logic behind hipster love of the Moleskine is as follows: if one was to purchase a similar model Fender Stratocaster to that of Jimi Hendrix, one is immediately Jimi Hendrix. That's right, Moleskine advertisers have laid the false claim of being the choice of past literary giants, and hipsters have lapped it up and then some.

Ironic trucker cap — The trucker cap has single-handedly popularised the modern use of the word 'douche', and helped millions of people understand the definition of a douche. While this faux-cheapo accessory is poison to the eye, it remains an important method of signpost when separating the douches from the non-douches.

Keffiyeh — This gender-neutral headdress borrowed from Palestinian culture is a unique stylistic incorporation, as well as an impassioned flying of the flag for liberal acceptance. The Keffiyeh is the official scarf of the hipster protest party.

Large headphones — Last decade, those who would grow into hipsters thought Dr. Dre was the more nasal member of Outkast. If at the time they had known that he was one of the founding fathers of hip-hop, they wouldn't have rolled their eyes. They swear. Now hipsters worship the man who discovered Eminem and Kendrick Lamar due to the fact that he creates the most professional consumer headphones on the market – Beats by Dre. "What do you mean they're overrated? They're red!" Hipsters with more vintage tastes get on the headphones-as-accessory bandwagon too: look out for big cans with wood panelling and anything that makes the wearer resemble a 60's radio producer.

EYEWEAR

If planning on insulting a hipster, throwing out the nickname 'four-eyes' will not yield the desired effect. In fact, they would most likely welcome the label as a compliment. Wearing frames is no longer lame, and even if it is lame it's lame in the cool way, and while hipsters are allowed to purchase numerous styles of eyewear, they are still bound by specific parameters.

Faux-spectacles — Hipsters have long been fighting against the barriers imposed by their perfect eyesight. A pair of glasses designed for reading or driving (the bigger and more ironic the better) can easily be fashioned into the perfect accessory by simply removing the lenses. (When trying to spot a hipster, the lack of reflective glint over the eyes is a dead giveaway.)

Wooden frames — Who doesn't enjoy feeling as if their eyewear has come straight out of woodshop? Wooden-framed glasses are all the rage with hipsters, and as long as they know how to stave off termites then this is one rustic fad that's likely to stick around.

Round frames — Some hipsters are more forward-thinking and opt to shunt conventional eyewear in favour of the more daring 'circular' shape. These hipsters are the crazy ones, the misfits, the round pegs in the square holes.

Ray-Ban Wayfarers — An iconic, hipster staple, the Ray-Ban Wayfarers come with the hipster orientation pack. Before a hipster enters a bar or coffee shop, their Ray-Bans are checked for authenticity, as there's nothing more frightening than a friend with fake Wayfarers.

Faux-spectacles

Wooden frames

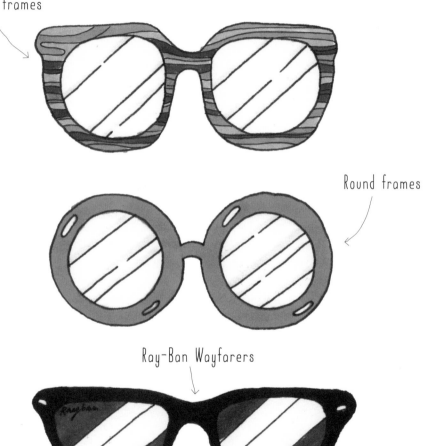

Round frames

Ray-Ban Wayfarers

MALE HIPSTER HAIRSTYLES

It's not easy to find a salon that deals solely in hipster 'dos, so until they start popping up, the general public must remain vigilant if they are going to keep up with what's considered a hipster hairstyle. Here are a few to get you started:

The man-bun — The man-bun is a carefully constructed whimsical pile of hair gracing the top of a hipster's head. The level of skill required to gather a significant bun while leaving the right number of loose hair-flicks is significant; therefore, a fair amount of a man-bun-sporting hipster's time is devoted to daily practice.

The Hitler-youth cut — The official haircut of WWII ethnic cleansing, this 'do has been appropriated by the male hipster with wild abandon. Another style that requires up to a tonne of hair product per year, it comprises shaved sides, long and slick hair with pomade on top.

The pompadour — If Johnny Cash awoke from the grave and wandered into a particular nook of a hipster hub, he'd no doubt think he was losing his mind, as every second male would bare his signature gelled, unparted quaff of a hairstyle.

The mountain-man mane — Paired with a beard, this long hairstyle wouldn't be unwelcome on the cover of a romantic seafaring novel. This versatile 'do is also compatible with the aforementioned man-bun.

The man-bun stays high up
on the head

Loose ends
of hair
deliberately
placed

Bald perfection

The 'Zooey'

Bright pastels

The messy shag

Vintage 'do

FEMALE HIPSTER HAIRSTYLES

Compared to male hipster hairdos, female dome-art is a whole different tub of styling wax. The following hairstyles could easily go out of fashion by the time you've finished reading this page, so keep your eyes peeled.

Pastel hair — Though many hipsters swear by all-things-earthy, a branch of hipsters have taken to radical hair dying. Bright, pastel colours not only catch the eye of passers-by, but also doubles as a handy hands-free night light.

The Zooey Deschanel — A classic hipster hairstyle of long, layered hair with long bangs, modelled on the indie-come-mainstream hipster starlet and Manic Pixie Dream Girl Zooey Deschanel.

Messy shag — Like the man-bun, the messy shag is not as easy to achieve as its name suggests. One cannot simply tussle one's hair into a shag or – God forbid – rely on actual bed-hair, as both a specially layered cut as well as a rare blow-drying technique are required.

The Pinterest braid — A popular pastime is to post one's braided hairstyle to Pinterest. This may sound simple, but a braid isn't merely a braid – for it to be Pinterest-worthy it must be insanely complicated. If a hipster is looking to attract swarms of fellow braiders, then they'd be wise to create a quirky how-to video tutorial.

Retro hairstyles — This is where female hipsters are allowed the freedom to cut loose. Here, they can choose from a number of vintage 'dos, as long as they can provide a date-stamped magazine clipping that proves its authenticity.

No hair — More recently, some female hipsters have opted to go commando up top. This could be a reaction to the hair-centralism of their male counterparts, or merely an idea inspired by Charlize Theron's character in *Mad Max: Fury Road*. Whichever way you shave it, this army of bald, badass hipsters is growing.

BEARDS

Way back when, Copernicus claimed that our earth and everything in it orbits the sun. The hipster community has since formed their own blinding energy source around which all things hipster revolve: the beard.

The difference between your everyday beard and a glorious hipster beard can be likened to the difference between a warm ten-dollar cask of Chardonnay and a bottle of Domaine Leflaive Montrachet Grand Cru at optimal drinking temperature.

Your everyday beard is merely a clump of dead cells, whereby the hipster beard is a living, breathing manstallation; a vital work of visual art that must be treated as such – with meticulousness, tenderness and the utmost respect.

The hipster beard is sculpted, symmetrical and over an inch thick. The most popular styles include the extended Van Dyke (a longer goatee that incorporates the moustache), the Hollywoodian (a longer goatee that doesn't connect to the sideburns), the full beard, and the Garibaldi (a puffier, fuller beard).

Hipsters can tweak their facial hedge as their signature style dictates. Whether sculpting the beard's tip into an interesting shape, sprucing-up the beard with a flower or vintage brooch, or breaking up the face with a toothpick or piece of hay, the hipster beard is an extension of the hipster's individuality.

A handy scale against which you can measure the quality of a hipster's beard is somewhere between a lumberjack and a member of ZZ Top.

Hipster beard

Not a hipster beard

The Handlebar

The Dali

The Horseshoe

The thicker Fu Manchu

Freestyle

MOUSTACHES

All hail the surface area between the nose and the upper-lip. Fall to the ripped-knee of your skinny jeans and bow your head to the narrow curvature of fertile skin, designed to give bloom to that wondrous flank of hair we call – the moustache.

The hipster moustache comes in various styles, and can either stand alone or with a beard. If a budding hipster enters a 50's-style barber for mo-maintenance, they will no doubt have memorised the following list:

The handlebar — The most common mustachioed hipster will don this particular style – where both sides of the 'do flick upwards into a small wave. This moustache reminds one of a saloon owner or silent-film projectionist.

The Dali — This moustache comes with the added bonus of giving the hipster the ability to mention its cultural inspiration. Named after famed crackpot artist Salvador Dali, this sleek, gelled lady-tickler resembles an upside-down pair of overdone eyebrows.

The horseshoe — Misleading in name, the horseshoe is more like a squared-off, upside-down U. Unbroken and thick, when worn without a beard it lends the hipster the air of disgruntled Wild West sheriff or unicycle inventor.

The thicker Fu Manchu — Two hairy waterfalls cascade from either side of the upper lip, caressing the sides of the mouth and resting at the chin. A fusion of Eastern and Western sensibilities.

Freestyle — Some hipsters prefer to trim outside the square and sculpt something more abstract. This is fine, as long as it's shapely and manicured, as one wouldn't want to give the impression of an unintentional moustache.

FACIAL HAIR MAINTENANCE

Leaving facial hair to grow into a beard and/or moustache is only part of the journey. In order for face fluff to earn the hipster wrist stamp, it should exist in an unbroken state of perfection. Here are some accessories of choice:

Hand mirror or iPhone camera — It goes without saying that hipsters lead busy lives and, therefore, are usually on the move. While most are experts at catching a quick glimpse of themselves in any number of reflective surfaces throughout the city, it's also imperative that they have ready access to either a mirror or their iPhone camera, as random reflective surfaces are prone to inaccuracy.

Beard oil — Not to be confused with oil that secretes from the face, beard oil is a product dedicated to ensuring that the hipster's beard and moustache hair remains lustrous and in tip-top shape. This ingenious liquid moisturises the facial hair as well as the skin underneath, and ensures that the face remains sweet on the nose and dandruff-free.

Beard comb — As bearded hipsters are recommended a tri-hourly re-combing of their morning sculpt, they like to spend a decent amount of money on a sturdy metal comb, and preferably one that's been designed and handcrafted by a bearded artisan.

Moustache wax — What guy doesn't want a thick, sticky substance between their nostrils and top lip? What partner doesn't want to taste the sweet tang of moustache wax upon a loving kiss?

Moustache comb — Don't even think of comparing it to a beard comb.

Moustache comb
(NB: totally different
from a beard comb)

It's important to
keep a regular check
on facial hair (and
offer updates)

Beard oil,
preferably organic

Beard comb

NATURAL HABITATS

COFFEE SHOPS

You can use a variety of metrics to measure how likely you are to spot a hipster at a particular coffee shop.

Square-footage — The smaller the establishment, the better. Tiny spaces lend an air of exclusivity. If a customer is able to stand in the middle of the space and touch opposing walls, they're onto a winner.

Seating — The less comfortable, the better. Nobody current wants to enjoy their chai on a common, ergonomically-effective chair. Filling a café with primary-school seating, milk crates, apple boxes or tree stumps ensures that patrons park their asses in style.

Barista — The more expansive their knowledge – and appreciation – of coffee, the better. Many mislabel the hipster barista as pretentious, when really they are a master of craft who understands that 99% of the sipping public is willfully ignorant. This skillful artisan is resigned to the fact that your coffee choice includes ingredients (such as milk) that interfere with the purity of the beans and the effort gone into the grind and that no one but them will understand why they have to charge $14 for their cold brew pour over.

Décor — The shabbier-looking, the better. No hipster proprietor would waste money on expensive interior design when they could put that money towards higher-quality steel-cut oats. Or at least, that's how it should appear. A café should ideally resemble someone's neglected backyard or a Victorian-era chemistry lab. Exposed foundations and stripped walls are completely acceptable, as long as they're cited as intentional design choices.

Breadboards — The great thing about moving past the restrictiveness of ceramic plates and towards the earthy charm of the breadboard, is that your food takes on an interesting woody aftertaste. Plus, who doesn't want to eat on something that contains grooves and crevices that potentially collect food, detergent and saliva?

The less comfortable the seating arrangements,
the more hipster the establishment

BARS

Directions to The Tin Box Bar: "You know The Rutherford Hotel? Well, ten or fifteen blocks from there, you turn left at the postbox, then left again at the elm tree into an alley that looks like a driveway. Follow that down until you see a gate with a replica vintage anchor attached to it. Go through the gate and past a row of dumpsters until you reach the rear of a small brick building. You should see a light coming from a set of descending stairs. There's no sign."

The hipster bar cannot be easily found, or at least that's what it says on Yelp next to the clearly marked map. If you're sitting in a greasy food court and you clock a group of young, bearded and tattooed faux-lumberjacks, chances are they're walking through the back of a sushi shop to the little-known whiskey bar that runs underneath. If you were to tail them and remain unnoticed, you might actually catch a glimpse of the establishment – a self-conscious mix of saloon and roadside diner where hot mixologists try not to spill moustache wax in their works of liquid art, or as we call them, cocktails. A bluegrass, country or folk band will play from an awkward part of the space, or an indie DJ will run an eclectic playlist from his or her MacBook.

Though most of these establishments boast food menus, such lists are arguably redundant, as, at any time a group could easily sit down without a menu and say "I'll have the kale chips, the kimchi pork slider, and the jalapeño poppers", without batting an eyelid.

Another sign that you're passing a hipster bar is if a bunch of hipsters are lined up outside a former fruit shop or butcher. Hipsters love to confuse everyday patrons by retaining the façade of the shop's former owners, oblivious to the fact that they might be debasing the legacies of retired small-business owners.

SMALL GALLERY OPENINGS

"Come down to the Create Or Die Gallery for Jacob Stonefish's premiere collection of framed phlegm entitled 'Me & My Tar'. The chain-smoking son of two cardio-vascular surgeons, this conceptual artist has used these smatterings of black spit to comment on the fact that smoking is, like, bad for people... or something. It's legit. Be there."

If you were to walk through the hipster hub of one of several renowned cities on a Friday or Saturday night, and you happened to peer down one of several dank alleyways, you'd no doubt see a brightly lit bustle of youths spilling out of a small gallery space. These cultural boffins never actually notice the art, but rather gather in small groups, gratis-sponsored beer in hand, and discuss other small gallery openings they've attended of late.

Even though the artistic work goes unnoticed, hipsters are savvy enough to wield the words 'dark', 'ephemeral', 'visceral', 'brave' and 'confronting' at random increments throughout the opening.

Constantly updating social media is vital to the music festival experience

MUSIC FESTIVALS

Woodstock. Monterey. Lollapalooza. Hipsters have scoured the most significant music festivals throughout history and mashed-up the most relevant aspects of each cultural shift into a new vibe.

Understanding how modern music festivals work is relatively straightforward:

The music is arbitrary — Hipsters know that musical genres are a thing of the past. Not only does one require an eclectic taste, but they also need to be aware that everyone's collaborating with everyone these days, so forcing music into such restrictive compartments is like, literally way judgmental. Who's on the bill is unimportant (apart from when discussing thoughts on the line-up with other hipsters); it's all about the vibe. As nobody is really listening to the music, they are free to turn away from the band and face their friends' cameras.

Phones are mandatory — Hipsters know that every moment of a music festival should be captured from all angles, so while walking between stages they stop at fifty-foot increments to take a meticulously constructed group photo that suggests they've just discovered fun for the first time. During performances, snaps of the hipster in the foreground and the act in the background are *de rigueur*, and are uploaded to social media within thirty seconds of photographing.

The festival vibe — When hipsters are old and grey, they want to look back at pictures from their youth with fondness and appreciation. Therefore, festival-goers have baked a cake that's part-hippie, part-country, part-raver, part-rocker and part-hip-hopper – all slathered in a new-age sheen. They sit in huddled groups on grassy hills, all waify and communal and free, as they orchestrate slick, everlasting memories.

POP-UPS

Entrepreneurs of previous generations lucky enough to run successful small businesses spent years cultivating the loyalty of the community. They'd fight through initial years of debilitating financial loss in order to grow a steady roster of customers, and then eventually settle for breaking even, or if lucky, a small annual profit.

No longer is a shop a fixed labour-of-love, thanks to the pop-up. Pop-ups are the shifty travelling salesman of the retail world – appearing out of nowhere, making as much money as the timeframe allows, then moving onto greener pastures. It's a great fit for the entrepreneurial, yet non-committal hipster. And as for the hipster public, the draw-card of a pop-up is exclusivity; hipsters only have a limited time to pop in to a pop-up, and if they don't make it, they might miss out on getting in on a new trend at the ground level, which means they'll also miss out on bragging potential.

In order to raise awareness of the pop-up, hipsters take to social media to whip their counterparts into such fervor that they pre-emptively agree to attend. These advertisements are usually accompanied with warnings of lengthy queues and limited capacity, in order to draw larger crowds.

Pop-ups are usually restaurants or clothing stores, but if a hipster hasn't enough money to invest in stock, they can easily just use the shop front as an extended yard sale.

CREATIVE CO-OPS

A graphic designer, a web designer, and a video editor walk into a bar...

...and convert it into an open-plan creative co-working space. These 'creatives' set up ten desks in a space fit for six, then advertise on social media to fill the other spots with other Mac users and charge a weekly rate that renders their own share of the rent redundant. They argue over whose contact will paint the street-art mural on the exterior wall, and give the place a name like 'The Factory', 'The Control Room' or 'CommuSpace'.

Each member of the co-op will arrive at various stages throughout the day and either dabble in their own freelance work – which is usually a pamphlet for a friends' gig, cover art or video clip for a friend's band, or a logo for a friend's company – or search job sites for freelance work. Ultimately, for whatever the space is being used, it will end up a place for its members to hold warehouse parties.

If a creative co-op member is asked what they do, they will inevitably say some version of 'I make content'. Content is a word that encompasses everything from online instructional videos to cat memes. The meaning and relevance of the content is irrelevant, as long as it garners likes and shares. In fact, it could be said that hipster creative co-ops, if they are 'co-operative' to any extent, are united in a hunt for the ad revenue accumulated from the likes and shares of internet content.

WAREHOUSE LIVING

"Room-mate wanted: huge warehouse space separated (with movable partitions) into seven bedrooms. Share with a 'family' of ten (four couples, two singles) creatives, male and female, gay and straight, all aged between 20–30. Like to keep the house looking slick, but on weekends will clear everything out and host the odd open-mic night or protest party. Open-minded creatives preferable. Pets welcome."

There's no more chilled abode than a warehouse or open-plan loft, as it gives the feel of being in New York without having to actually be there. But this choice of residence isn't purely superficial, as hipsters need an abundance of space for all the musical instruments and camera equipment they're never going to use.

Common features of a hipster warehouse residence include: a portion of a wall set up as a photographic studio; a communal table strewn with Apple products and take-away coffee cups; a retro arcade game either in-use or used as a coffee table; a hollow CRT television that was used as a massive candle-holder and is now an artwork of oozing wax; an overpriced purchase from a street-art gallery; and a retro fridge covered in Polaroids from music festivals.

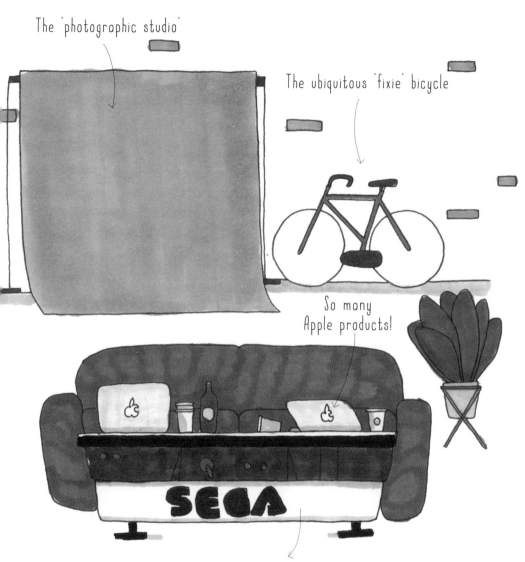

The 'photographic studio'

The ubiquitous 'fixie' bicycle

So many
Apple products!

A very hipster coffee table

Man-bun

Talent is no barrier to
a successful open-mic night

OPEN-MIC NIGHTS

A young hipster takes to a vintage microphone and straightens her lens-less, wooden frames before pulling out a torn piece of Moleskine notebook paper. She clears her throat and signals to the lighting guy, who also happens to be one of her friends, until she's under a narrow spotlight.

"Can I just say how legit awesome it is to be surrounded by people who just really, really love words, dude."

(Rapturous applause)

Whether poetry, singer–songwriter or performance art night at the local warehouse-conversion watering hole, attendees are guaranteed their cover-charge's worth and then some. The best thing about open-mic nights is their inclusiveness – anyone with any degree of talent can book a slot and show their stuff, no matter how hard they've worked or carefully they've planned leading up to the gig.

If a fly-on-the-wall were to give an eyewitness account of an average week on a tiny hipster stage, it'd most likely include entertainment in the vein of the following:

☐ Freestyle poems about labias.

☐ Overwritten personal short stories.

☐ Erotic fan-fiction readings involving Harry Potter characters.

☐ Songs about forests and highways.

☐ Songs that seem to be about love but are really about the sociopathic tendencies of the songwriter.

☐ A musician that owes his or her sound to Johnny Cash.

☐ Another musician that owes his or her sound to Johnny Cash.

☐ Another musician that owes his or her sound to Johnny Cash and early Kanye West.

☐ Self-deprecating white rap ridden with pop-cultural references.

FARM WEDDINGS

Marriages that take place in conventional, practical locations like religious structures or secular function halls are rituals for other, less-adventurous subcultures. Why consider guest expenditure or convenience when they can be forced to find a way to a distant country location and stay overnight in a charming little (extortionate) bed and breakfast?

Though guests might have to fork out a few weeks' rent in order to fund the trip and wedding gift, they must remember it's all in the name of someone else's special day. If a hipster couple wants to wake up on the morning of their nuptials to the smell of alpaca manure, then they have every right to wake up on the morning of their nuptials to the smell of alpaca manure.

The reception of a hipster farm wedding would no doubt boast a restored barn, a derivative bluegrass band, novelty prop-chocked photo-booth, and an ocean of bowties, braces and 1950s tulle.

Farm animals can add authenticity
to a hipster wedding

~ IMPORTANT ISSUE !!! ~

🕐 NOW

📍 Federation Square

⬛ Write Post | ⬛ Add Photo/Question

Write something...

20 FRiends are attending

482   100   1213
going   maybe invited

🏠 KORA ALLEN   ∨

OMG ~ GET DOWN HERE RN! 😠

PROTEST PARTIES

History has shown us that a group of passionate, unrelenting folk can unite in protest and change the course of the future for the better. Photographic records of dissent at The Berlin Wall, Tiananmen Square and the 2004 Ukrainian Presidential election (leading to the 'Orange Revolution') reveal the emotional power and startling strength that comes in numbers. These freedom fighters charge forward knowing full well the life-threatening dangers they might encounter along the way.

For the hipster, these protests are unnecessarily serious, and drag out for way too long. They don't see the point of growing so in-your-face and heated, especially if the protest falls on a nice, sunny day. No matter the specifics of the issue in question, protest marches are really about clever pun-based signs, low-impact exercise and warehouse after-parties.

To stay informed, hipsters turn to Facebook, where they assess the importance of an issue based on how many of their friends are attending the protest. After each protest, photos are uploaded to social media, and if it weren't for the picket signs one might think these dissenters were holding a highly disorganised fashion parade.

BEHAVIOUR

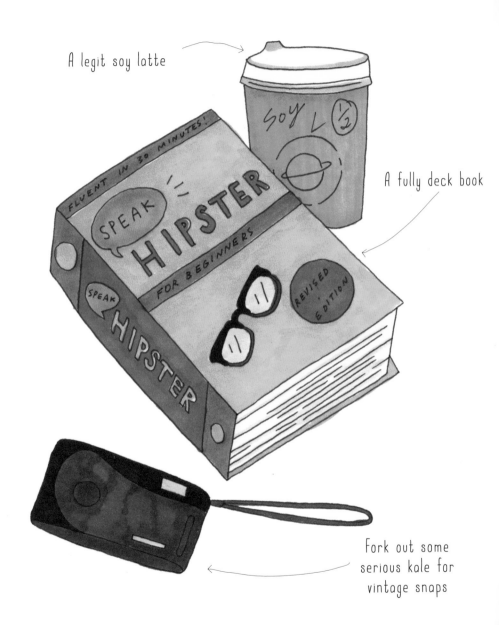

A legit soy latte

A fully deck book

Fork out some serious kale for vintage snaps

LANGUAGE

New hipster words appear regularly and spread throughout the subculture quicker than an advanced airborne disease in Africa. By the time you read this book, most of these will have been replaced with words of which you've never heard and therefore just don't understand.

Deck — Not to be confused with a full set of playing cards, a part of a ship, or the sheltered platform at the rear of your parent's beach house, hipsters use the word 'deck' to describe the aesthetically pleasing. "Did you see Marty added a miniature vintage car to the elastic of his man-bun? It looked deck."

Legit — What began as a way hipsters confirm the truth to other hipsters, this contraction of 'legitimate' is now a multi-purpose word used on many occasions throughout a conversation. "How are you, legit?" (How are you, really?) "I'm legit, thanks." (I'm good thanks.) "Legit, legit." (Acknowledgement, acknowledgement.)

Literally — Hipsters are known to increase the effectiveness of their sentences by inviting the word 'literally' where it's not wanted. "Coachella was so hot my face was literally melting."; "Kings of Leon have literally jumped the shark."; "I am literally having sex with the word 'literally'."

Kale — If a hipster asks "Can you slip me some kale?" don't reach for the crisper. A common source of confusion, as hipsters are also rhapsodic about the vegetable of the same name, but in this case the hipster is referring to 'kale' as money – an ironic reference to the term 'greenback' as slang for a dollar bill.

Indie — If a hipster is asked what genre of music, film or games they enjoy, no doubt one of them will answer 'indie'. If one were to probe further and enquire as to the stylistic conventions that make up the term 'indie', one would receive a blank stare, as 'indie' is a catch-all term to describe "stuff I like, ie, cool stuff," as opposed to its original reference to independent methods of distribution and production.

IRONY

It's common knowledge that hipsters aren't fantastic at placing the word 'irony' in its correct context, but so is the fact that incessant use of the word 'irony' is integral to the hipster experience. Therefore, instead of falling to outdated ways, hipsters are keeping up with the fluidity of language and redefining the word for the now, in the hope that they no longer have to follow every mention of the word with the following qualifying half-sentence:

"...ironic in an Alanis-Morissette kinda way."

Old Definition In order to properly digest the new definition, lets take a look at what irony meant when it was a lowly literary device.

Irony *The use of words to convey a meaning that is the opposite of its literal meaning.*

For example: "I named my sausage dog 'Stiltz'." (Irony: the dog is literally low to the ground, and the owner has chosen a name that suggests great height, which is the opposite meaning.)

Or: "I wrote a book that celebrates the rarity and originality of the modern hipster" (despite the fact they are a mainstream subculture).

New Definition

Irony Saying, doing and wearing things that you know are uncool because it's hilarious.

For example: "I'm wearing a well-ironic Golden Girls shirt to the protest party on Saturday."

Or: "I love Jethro Tull, in an ironic kind of way, of course."

While this new definition has its fair share of issues, in the long run its addition to our lexicon will make things easier for everyone.

A well-ironic tee. Hilarious!

Creative thinking

Organic paint brush

Organic paint swatches

Organic chai

BEING SEEN AS CREATIVE

"I'm a creative. What does that mean? Um... well I kinda do a bit of graphic design, a bit of writing, bit of web-stuff. I can use Photoshop and Lightroom. But my first love is art. I post pictures of the beginnings of my drawings all the time, just so people know I'm about to create something. I swear, I don't sit there waiting for the post to get more likes, I finish every work. It's all about the work."

Most hipsters stand up for the rights of creative people. They understand the burden that comes with artistic talent, and rightly ridicule narrow-minded hard-working people who just don't understand that employment interferes with the artistic process. And besides, most hipsters are waiting to find out about a government grant or artistic residency that they're definitely going to receive pretty soon.

At one time, the world revered art that displayed visual ingenuity or spoke to new or universal truths. Works of art could give voice to the silenced, or closure to the traumatised. Hipsters know that times have changed, and that art is now more open to interpretation. It's perfectly acceptable to pursue an idea due to its potential to look cool or shock people, and then attribute meaning to it after the fact.

For example: a hipster asks her friends to post over their used make-up wipes. She likes the way they look like little round paint swatches. She goes on to attach each wipe to an individual canvas, hangs them in a small gallery space, then decides that the collection was created to defetishise the female face and reveal the superficiality of modern beauty standards.

And if a hipster runs out of ideas, they can take someone else's work and mash it up into something avant-garde, and call it homage. If questioned, they can always say "There are no original ideas, dude."

DJING

Eons ago – that is to say, less than a decade ago – the art of DJing was unnecessarily complicated. These mixmasters perfectly beat-matched tracks, chopped up samples and reorganised them into new works, and actually played their own compositions. These DJs worked behind decks made up of two-or-more turntables, manipulating a vast array of knobs, switches, dials and sliders like Beethoven conducting a symphony. They were innovators; their two hands doing the work of eight. It was all so unnecessarily showy.

Now, hipsters have revealed DJing for what it should be – the practice of compiling songs into a playlist and pressing play on a user-friendly device. The hipster DJ doesn't need knowledge of musical theory or history; they don't need samplers or effects racks, heck, they don't even need to know the names of the tracks in their playlist. All they need is access to iTunes, Spotify and an RCA-to-mini-jack audio cable.

The most important facet of the hipster DJ is their sartorial style. Chances are that every DJ's playlist will end up exactly the same, so it's imperative that they adopt a signature, marketable look. Adding gimmickry gives any budding DJ a leg-up – the DJ who sucks on a sequined pacifier, or who wears subversive political singlets and novelty sunglasses, or who performs with sharpened nipple-tassels, is more likely to break into the scene. While the art of DJing couldn't be more simple, nailing an original DJ look takes more forethought.

Organic fruit

Organic vegetables

Organic tattoos?

ORGANIC LIVING

The most important sequence of seven letters since 'science' – 'organic' anything is the single solution to Earth's every ill. If you discovered the truth about non-organic living you'd experience an immediate existential crisis – you'd curl up in a corner and wonder whether you might already be dead.

But you're not dead. There's still time to grow, and you can start by growing organic. Sure, buying organic is awesome, but if you really want to escape the spotty reliability of farmers' markets, y'all best get your seed on.

Away from the world of pesticides and hormones, hipsters can be easily spotted at organic supermarkets, organic clothing stores, organic toyshops, organic dry-cleaners and organic banks.

A way to discern an organic from a hellish and poisonous establishment is to check its extent of common signifiers such as hessian, repurposed warehouse pallets, and old wood.

CYCLING

Screw helmets. Skull-protection is for squares and city couriers. And screw cycling gear. Lycra is for 80's costume parties. In Amsterdam, nobody wears a helmet or lycra; they dress like models out of winter-fashion catalogues and that's how every other city should be.

Along with the beard and skinny jeans, cycling completes the Holy Trinity of the genesis of modern hipsterdom. But there are specific guidelines. Hipster cyclists do not require the luxury of brakes or the ability to properly navigate hilly terrain with gears and, therefore, ride fixed-gear bicycles, or 'fixie-bikes' or 'fixies'. The drawcard of fixies is their lean aesthetic value, and the cooler and more vintage the fixie, the less secure the life of the hipster.

For the hipster fixie-biker, road rules need not apply. Cyclists are welcome to switch from concrete to bitumen without warning, tail cars and pedestrians, and lane-split cars waiting at red lights. They earn the right to protest the scarcity of bike lanes in the city, but then not actually use the lanes once implemented. After most rides, the fixie-bike rider will share a story about the evils of cars and drivers, then gladly catch an Uber to a gig that night.

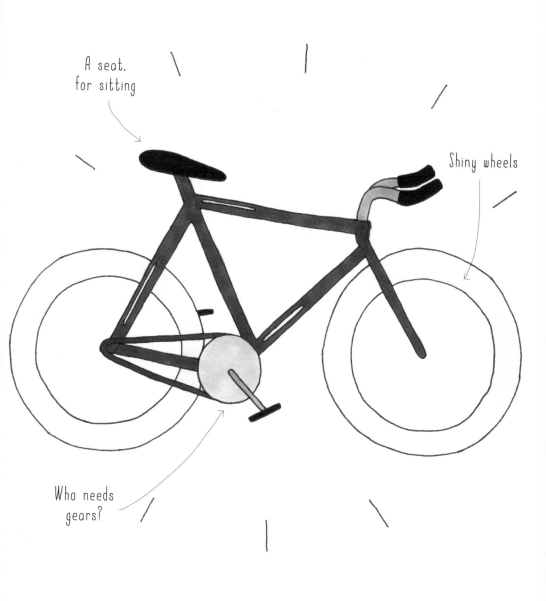

Classic 'selfie' #irony

If you didn't Instagram it,
did you even eat it?

INSTAGRAMMING

Social media is a fantastic platform to spot hipsters sharing the idiosyncrasies of their lifestyles with the rest of the world. While everybody hates an online narcissist, hipsters are able to get away with relentless sharing of personal content as long as each photo is accompanied by a self-aware comment or ironic hashtag. Of course, it also helps that Instagram has a cool, vintage-film appeal.

Food — If a hipster queues for the latest hybrid-pastry-obsession pop-up or visits an underground invite-only freegan dinner party, and nobody's around to see it, did it ever really happen? After ordering the most photogenic thing on the menu, eating takes a backseat to rearranging table-setting items into a formation that makes best use of the rule-of-thirds. Of course, true hipsters wouldn't dare use the totally mainstream in-app photo filters, instead they opt for the more indie VSCO Cam to add additional hipster appeal.

Selfies — It's important to note that hipsters don't post 'selfies'. A hipster 'self-portrait' is always accompanied by some kind of self-aware comment about the shamelessness of today's youth and a string of ironic hashtags. Adopting a mock duck-face can be a great way to show how superficial and vacuous you're not. #irony.

Street art — Nothing says 'street' like photos of a fresh graff or commissioned mural. Many hipsters – particularly those from wealthier families – will brave what they view as the more dangerous parts of their city, taking gritty snaps like scenes out of a Spike Lee Joint. These pictures are generally accompanied by the artist's name and a reference to their upcoming small gallery opening.

Kickstarter
Yesterday at 01:25

You won't believe how these guys have revolutionised the sock game.

Like   Comment   Share

You really won't believe the insane stuff that gets funded

CROWDFUNDING

"Thanks so much to the beautiful, wonderful people that have donated money to my upcoming short film 'Grandma'. For those of you who missed the last few posts, 'Grandma' is the quirky story of a young girl whose grandmother dies, told in part live action, part animation. So far we've raised $2,300 of the $5,000 we need to bring this whimsical and important tale to life. There are a bunch of incentives that get cooler the more you donate, such as DVD copies of the short film, signed DVD copies of the short film, and limited edition DVD copies of the short film including director's commentary. But even if you merely sacrifice your daily coffee and donate some spare change, the 'Grandma' team will love you forever! Thank you so much and all you donators are so beautiful!"

Gone are the days when creators were forced to work menial jobs in order to subsidise the pursuit of their dreams. Want to record your EP but couldn't be bothered saving for a few months? Crowdfund. Need to buy the yarn for your upcoming craftism street-mural? Crowdfund. Designed a new range of T-shirts branded with faded covers of classic movies but don't have access to a screenprinter? Crowdfund that puppy.

Hipsters now need only an idea (and a really cool video) and they can ask the world to take on the financial burden in return for a 'reward' that could easily be the door prize at a retirement home social. The only downside is that crowdfunding platforms like Kickstarter are highly competitive, so it can be difficult to raise the attention of the general public – but that's not too problematic as hipsters can easily take their Facebook friends on a daily guilt trip until the desired target is met.

CULTURE

ARTISAN CRAFTS

For the hipster crafter, an original work of art is not complete without a pithy pop-culture reference or wittily repurposing an everyday item with a vintage twist.

Here are a few examples of what might be sold on a hipster's Etsy page or from their artisan craft stall:

- ☐ Thrift store crockery stenciled with iconography from cult cinematic classics such as *Pulp Fiction* and *Vertigo*.
- ☐ Large shells from the beach painted to look like zombie faces; fake pieces of fruit painted to look like zombie faces; beanies knitted to look like zombie faces.
- ☐ Framed photos of street art that may or may not be the sellers' major work from conceptual art school.
- ☐ Vintage jewellery taken apart and tied into new pieces of vintage jewellery.
- ☐ A skull prop from a high-school production of Hamlet, covered in multicolour glitter countours.
- ☐ Lithographs and Lino prints of doctored brand logos.
- ☐ Burlap and twine wedding save-the-dates, hand-died with organic cola.
- ☐ Mason jars with various novelty handles.

Towards the end of market day, a hipster will often grow disheartened at the lack of interest in their labours-of-love that took a good half-day of backbreaking work to assemble. At this point, the hipster's friends and family can usually be relied on to purchase remaining stock in order to help the hipster regain some semblance of self.

Cult-film-inspired
hipster-style
crockery

Vintage jewellery
fashioned into
'vintage jewellery'

Framed street art

Mason jars with
hilarious novelty
handles

Mason jar

MASON JARS

Any hipster establishment worth name-dropping knows that regular conical glassware is predictable, uninspired and aesthetically poisonous. Whether they're serving their Chopin Vodka in Art-Deco peppershakers, or double ristrettos in oversized novelty thimbles, you'll be able to assess the hipsterness of a bar or café by how they choose to package their liquids. And of course, the most hipster beverage receptacle remains the completely impractical mason jar.

The mason jar differs from your stock-standard jar, in that the former is used in the preservation of organic fruit and vegetables. It boasts a wide mouth, and its rivets make a nifty resting place for a hipster's chin-rug.

This popular drink container harks back to a time when folk entered bars through saloon doors and so imbues a drinking session with a sense of nostalgia, while – with the innovative addition of the handle – still remaining current.

Less prevalent hipster-appealing beverage-ware – yet equally ingenious – includes small vases, large decorative egg cups and the base sections of Russian matryoshka dolls.

NEW THINGS MADE TO LOOK OLD

Most human beings fortunate enough to shop outside necessity covet the latest, most futuristic-looking technology. They marvel at the exponential leaps and bounds made by man and long to be a part of society's forward propulsion.

These people have cold dead hearts and no semblance of style.

Hipsters, however, are aware that 60s and 70s technology looked the coolest, and even though most hipsters were born well after 1980, they know that we just don't make things like we used to.

But what we can do is manufacture products made to look like something out of another era. Not wanting to sacrifice the capabilities of modern technology for the inconvenience that comes with actual vintage items (such as buying and processing film and not being able to connect your audio device to iTunes), a hipster can be easily spotted sporting an expensive, full HD-capable digital camera designed to look like a cheap Soviet-era SLR, or playing their favourite Spotify playlist through speakers embedded into a vintage suitcase.

This preference extends to leather satchels, vintage-style bicycles, wooden turntables, landline telephone mobile handsets, cassette tape iPhone covers and energy-inefficient large-filament light globes.

Packaging is *everything*

If you're going to make a non-meta comedy that's taken seriously, it better be in-your-face. *Girls* is so *real*, and so *raw*. To the hipster, Lena Dunham is a genius and a champion of gratuitous nudity. *Girls* shows the world that hipsters are people too — that they're merely moving through life trying to figure out who they are.

Though some hipsters find the self-awareness of *Portlandia* a little close to home, most are able to justify their love. For starters, the show stars iconic hipster Carrie Brownstein, who nobody knows is a member of the most unknown amaze band Sleater-Kinney. If the Queen of hipsterdom is able to poke fun at herself, then hipsters can too.

TV

Hipsters know that there's no longer any point using the term 'television shows'. Nobody owns a TV anymore, unless they're using an old, fat CRT monitor as an art piece or backyard stool. Now it's all about watching 'content', and the scope of a hipster's appreciation of televisual products is strictly defined.

Prestige drama — A simple way to know if a drama is worth watching is if the content is preceded by the animated HBO logo, but a real hipster can be identified when citing the channel's status as being overtaken by online content-makers such as Netflix and Amazon. It's not imperative that hipsters watch these shows, but they will be sure to point out whether or not they were made by the creator of *The Wire* or *Breaking Bad*. It's also handy to look out for anyone gushing over *Twin Peaks*, even if they didn't get through the first episode.

Meta-comedy — Calling content 'meta' is another way of saying it's a show that shows awareness of the fact it's a show. Winking at the audience is clever, and so hipsters love to quote *Community* or *Family Guy* or *Arrested Development*. Becoming part of a show's in-joke is key, so for a hipster, being able to turn to their friends and let them know what's a reference, parody, or bit of knowingness, is an unparalleled feeling.

FILM

Apart from the odd legit comic book adaptation or Pixar film, modern mainstream films are for multiplex-attending, suburban conservatives. Hipsters know filmmaking is serious, credible business, and cannot fathom why the general public sets such base expectations when it comes to cinematic entertainment. If an undercover cop were to infiltrate a warehouse apartment full of hipsters in order to bring them down from the inside, he or she would need decent knowledge of the following cinematic realms:

Mumblecore — A good way to assess the originality and hipster-appropriateness of a movie is by taking a close look at its dialogue. The more characters spit self-aware, sarcastic dialogue full of outlandish metaphors, witty repartee, and rapid-fire use of 'like' and 'whatever' (and usually all improvised), the more successful the journey.

Other helpful yardsticks in discerning a film's worth include: a super low production budget that makes the film look super low budget; the use of non-professional 'actors'; cuts in the narrative to animated or stop-motion sequences; plots about self-actualisation and overcoming depression; niche pop-cultural references; and a soundtrack comprised of melancholy songs from an indie solo-artist.

Names to drop: Andrew Bujalski, Joe Swanberg, Lynn Shelton, Greta Gerwig, The Duplass Brothers, Lena Dunham.

Films to drop: Funny Ha Ha, Baghead, The Puffy Chair, Humpday, Tiny Furniture, Frances Ha.

If you know this is an illustration from Wes Anderson's *The Royal Tenenbaums*, you may be a hipster

Hipsters love *The Neverending Story*

The Criterion Collection — Navigating the cinematic world in order to find a legit film can be as disorienting as choosing the right shade of green smoothie. Luckily, a selection of critically adored darlings has been made for you under the esteemed umbrella of 'The Criterion Collection'. This careful curation of artistic glory helps a hipster complete the sentence "Oh, yeah I've seen that. It's great. But have you seen [X]?" (NB: It's not important that you've seen [X], as long as you can cite the name of the director.)

Films to drop: Breathless, The 400 Blows, 8½, The Bicycle Thief, Citizen Kane, Eternal Sunshine Of The Spotless Mind, Annie Hall, M, La Strada.

David Lynch and Wes Anderson — Though a hipster doesn't need an invitation to regale anyone with their knowledge of quirky independent cinema, two filmmakers are undisputed masters of the form.

"David Lynch is the most pure filmmaker to have ever graced our earth, due to him like being so, like, weird and like, legit not giving a damn. I adore everything he's made: *Twin Peaks*, and *Mulholland Drive*, and … anyway I can't wait for the *Twin Peaks* reboot. Did you know Lynch is into transcendental meditation?"

"Wes Anderson is a genius and the reason I chose to apply for film school. I'm heavily influenced by his symmetrical, choreographed cinematography and his hyper-realistic production design. He proves that visual quirks are the key to filmmaking, and my latest film *The Pomeranian Butler* is part-homage to his ongoing legacy. The promotional material boasts the same font as the poster from *Where The Wild Things Are*."

80's Films — Everyone knows popular films suck soggy popcorn, with the exception of popular films made in the 80s, such as kids' fantasy films and tacky-cool comedies starring members of the brat pack.

Names to drop: Molly Ringwald, Robin Wright, Rob Lowe, Judd Nelson, Matthew Broderick, Jim Henson, Jennifer Connolly, Cary Elwes, Mandy Patinkin, John Hughes.

Films to drop: The Princess Bride, Pretty In Pink, Labyrinth, Ferris Bueller's Day Off, The Dark Crystal, The Neverending Story, The Breakfast Club, The Goonies.

BEAT LITERATURE

Every hipster needs to memorise the following ~~Steve Jobs~~ Jack Kerouac quote so they can post it on social media and imply it's about them:

"Here's to the crazy ones. The misfits. The Rebels. The Troublemakers. The round pegs in the square holes. The ones who see things differently."

The Beat Generation were a bunch of vain, narcissistic chauvinists who mythologised road trips across the USA into near-religious status. Hipsters love to carry around a dog-eared copy of Jack Kerouac's *On The Road*, regardless of whether or not it was them that did the dog-ear'ing.

Though the free and individualistic philosophies that fuel works such as *On the Road* are important for the hipster to have in the back of their mind in case it comes up in future conversation, the real draw-card is the aesthetic of the time period. Male hipsters are known to draw inspiration from the character of Dean Moriarty, and female hipsters long for the Marylou look (especially as immortalised by vampire-turned-hipster Kristen Stewart in the 2012 film adaptation).

For hipsters, discussing any Beat novel other than *On The Road* is pointless, as nobody comes close to Kerouac (and they wouldn't know anything about them anyway).

A dog-eared copy of *On the Road*
adds to hipster cred

A typical weekend haul for a hipster

FLEETWOOD MAC

FLEETWOOD MAC

Leather satchel

VINYL RECORDS

"Blew most of my rent on records this morning. Some deck finds, legit. A Japanese copy of Johnny Cash's *Story Songs of Trains and Rivers*, a few Dylans, a Robert Johnson, and a pristine copy of 'Do The Bartman' (just for LOLZ), as well as a few more with hilarious retro cover photos. Looking forward to giving these a spin!"

CD's are dead. Tapes are kinda cool, but just in a fun kind of way. File formats can be sweet if compressed at a high bit rate. But to the hipster, everything sounds better on vinyl. Cash sounds better on vinyl, Mumford and Sons sound better on vinyl – in fact, even the piercing silence of outer space heard from the surface of the moon sounds better on vinyl.

On a Saturday or Sunday morning, hipsters can be spotted zipping from record store to record store, stacking LP after LP after 12-inch after 12-inch into their Herschel backpacks. Particularly obscure or ironic finds are posted on social media before being slotted into a growing collection, arranged alphabetically in stacks of milk crates or an eight-sectioned storage unit from Ikea.

In most cases a hipster's record collection does not necessitate turntable ownership, but in the rare instance that they do own a record player (modern but designed to look like a 1970s original), a cursory listen usually occurs shortly after procurement; however, the contents of the record generally takes a backseat to the process of adding to the collection.

FLEETWOOD MAC

"Last night I went on a date with a guy who didn't know Fleetwood Mac. At first I thought he was joking when he said he didn't know Fleetwood Mac, but when he confirmed that he actually didn't know Fleetwood Mac, I swear I Fleetwood Mac'ed out of that Fleetwood Mac'ing place faster than you can say Fleetwood Mac."

The official band of the modern hipster, Fleetwood Mac is a band name that cannot be taken in vain, and even if it is, such opinions fall on deaf ears. While the validity and worth of all art is considered subjective, Fleetwood Mac falls in to no such shades of grey. They are unequivocally great, and anyone who disagrees either doesn't appreciate music or is a pathetic contrarian.

Never press a hipster for the specifics when it comes to their love of the Mac. If they announce that Fleetwood Mac only released one album called *Rumours*, it's best to let it go. If they refer to Stevie Nicks as a male and retell the inter-band relationship woes as a same-sex love triangle, there's nothing you can do to change their mind.

If you were on the heartless side of humanity, you could ask a hipster to recite the lyrics to a Fleetwood Mac song that isn't 'Dreams', but nobody's that cruel.

Never discuss Fleetwood Mac in
anything other than glowing terms
around a hipster

STREET ART

Before the dawn of the modern hipster, street art was known as 'graffiti', and was synonymous with either gang-life or privileged 14-year-old school children with busy parents. Thanks to the subversive anonymous underground artist Banksy (you probably haven't heard of him, but check him out), art-on-the-street gained credibility and moved into the world of gallery shows and printed coffee table books, allowing the hipster community to embrace – and even partake in – this thriving artistic movement.

Scrawling a haphazard graffiti tag or piece is not only lacking in artistic talent, but it's brutish and disruptive to the community. Similarly, hurdling train-track fences and hanging off overpasses in order to communicate a socially relevant message is immature and unnecessarily dangerous.

Don't fret, as street art is now a cut above the street, bound by far greater aesthetic standards, and potentially a lucrative career choice. Hipsters no longer have to walk to more dangerous areas of town to clock a fine graff or mural; they can view them on lifestyle blogs and find guides to local street art in coffee shops and fashion boutiques. Most inner-city hipster havens include numerous commissioned walls, each far more important than the rights of the property owners. As spray-paint isn't organic, many hipsters opt for quirky mediums like yarn bombing, adhesive paste-ups, and recycled metals/plastics.

Novice street artists usually opt for stencils of iconic celebrities, mutated cartoon characters, 50's pin-up iconography and liberal propaganda.

Hipsters can often be spotted in
roadside diners (or venues made to
look like roadside diners)

AMERICANA

The hipster scene is chock-full of people who, a few years ago, couldn't give a damn about anything outside of the city, but recently, rural America and its earthy aspects has driven its pick-ups and horses deep into the subculture. Hipsters from gentrified US cities who previously turned their backs at any mention of middle/southern America, now embrace the iTunes-sponsored open road, and those from hipster hubs outside the US have followed suit.

Bluegrass, country and folk — Keeping in line with beards, music festivals and rustic aesthetics, hipsters who spent their teenage years listening to techno now swear by these twangy genres of music. Finally, it's no longer embarrassing to attend a hoedown, and the Holy Grail for the musical hipster is to become the next Joaquin Phoenix Johnny Cash.

Roadside diners — For hipster chefs, the ultimate venue is an inner city establishment that can be turned into something out of an *Archie* comic and serving up a menu of greasy, Southern-inspired food that includes fried chicken, gumbo, sliders and jalapeño poppers.

50's counter-culture — Romanticising the highway-road trip a la Jack Kerouac and the Beat poets is common practice amongst hipsters, mainly for the deck snaps taken along the way that are perfect for Instagram. Unfortunately, hipsters can look a little silly attempting to emulate their heroes driving Route 66 in a Prius rather than a Cadillac.

DIET

FREE FOOD OR BY-DONATION

"Okay, Martin, you go up to the chubby volunteer and distract her with your beard then me and Charlie will slip out the front door. Once you can sense that we've gone, ask for her number, and she'll be so dizzy from the whole thing that you'll be able to slip out too.

And if she happens to keep her eyes on you as you leave, just reach into your pocket and – with a closed fist – pretend to drop something in the donation box.

Now lets go buy some craft beer."

Hipsters in wait for inevitable fame or those busy riding the wave of self-discovery, aren't always flush with kale (not the vegetable version anyhow), so are forced to get a little creative. Luckily, if the line at the homeless food truck is too long or smelly, by-donation, municipality subsidised eateries are popping up all over the shop, both as pop-ups and non-pop-ups.

The idea is that you fork over your spare change after consuming a generous serving of (usually vegan) goodness, followed by a generous portion of a (usually vegan) dessert. If you're lucky, you might even get a second glass of chai. But sometimes, spare change is reserved for other aspects of the lifestyle, so a hipster is forced to rationalise their actions as a karmic IOU.

CRAFT BEER

While most philistines are clueless to the fact that beer bubbles beyond the scope of 'lager' and 'light', the hipster understands the veritable rainbow of artisanal flavours available at the most coveted bars and micro-breweries in town.

Here are some craft beer concoctions that have become hipster favourites:

Pumpkin-spiced ale — Take a pumpkin and four kinds of malt and spice it up until it tastes like rotting pie.

Coconut-curry beer — On a muggy day, there's nothing more refreshing than a mouthful of thick, sparkling curry water. Comes with the added bonus of eliminating the need to waste money on those curry-flavoured pretzels.

Oyster beer — Unsophisticated palates aren't able to embrace the slime, but hipsters know that shucking raw oysters right into a brew turns beer into a powerful aphrodisiac.

Chocolate beer — A great combination, as long as it's the product of a collab with one of Portland's finest artisanal chocolatiers and contains only hand-harvested raw organic cacao beans.

Sock beer — As most hipsters aren't fans of wearing socks, they use their pre-hipster purchases to brew a distinct kind of beer. The taste can be described as a malty fresh-cotton, with a blueberry finish.

Conceptual beer (rare) — Only a few – if any – establishments serve this particular flavour, partly due to the fact that it was an art major's final project. Customers are only served this brew if they are able to imagine the beer is there, even if it isn't.

For the hipster, a boutique brew is
the only acceptable type of beer

Pickle

PICKLES

You know those things your grandfather liked to eat out of the jar during *Jeopardy*? Those nubby green chunks with the texture of boiled cacti? Well your grandfather was more progressive than you thought.

The pickle is no longer restricted to the realm of country house pantries and craving-struck pregnant women. It's no longer the only ingredient stopping fast food burgers from being labelled as confectionery. Pickles have emerged as a hipster culinary obsession.

Hipsters who are into making their own pickles are no longer defensive about their choices. *Portlandia* poked knowing fun at the process and made it okay. Hipster picklers are now free to devote as much time as desired to soaking anything in as much vinegar as desired, and they do – emphatically.

It is rumoured that some hipsters get together for 'pickling parties' – events where they eat pickles and pickled foods; talk about pickles, pickling and pickled foods; and of course – pickle foods. As no layman has been lucky enough to attend a pickling party, we can't be sure exactly how much actual pickling eventuates. The mind boggles.

KALE, QUINOA AND CHIA

Hipsters are the Quentin Tarantinos of the food world; finding little known, yet internationally used, ingredients and turning them into the most sought after staples in town. The more exotic sounding the ingredient, the more likely it is to take catch on.

Kale — Not too long ago, kale was brussels sprouts' even uglier, even less popular distant cousin. In other words, it was a vegetable that those with functioning tastebuds avoided due to its foot-sweat-like properties. Now, kale is what spinach always wanted to be – a welcome addition to any plate and, when blended into a shake, the only way to start the day.

Quinoa — Why would anyone weigh themselves down with any version of rice when they can choose a grain that resembles microscopic larvae? This semi-translucent, unpronounceable hipster staple better be on the menu or the establishment will receive a highly scathing – and equally clever – Yelp review.

Chia — Not to be confused with chai, chia is a super seed that will continue to cure the hipster of any physical, mental or spiritual ailment, until the next miracle grain or seed pops to the surface.

Precious kale

Drip filter coffee

Kombucha

Small-batch whisky

ARTISAN SPIRIT~

Bespoke magazine

Chai

DRINKS

Beverage snobbery is rife among the hipster community, and with good reason. A direct line can be traced from a person's worth and the tipple they choose to introduce to their system. Hipster relationships are known to break down over the fine print of liquid-related legislation. Below is a small section of the hipster drinks menu.

Drip filter coffee — "If anyone touches instant coffee they are immediately barred from my Facebook and banished to the fiery belly of hell. Seriously, if you're going to be so hideously uncultured and suck on preservative-plagued synthetics, that's your prerogative. Your VISA application to flavour country has been unsuccessful. #coffeesnob #idontgiveadamnwhatyouthink."

Chai — If one was sitting on a bench on a busy street, and noticed a directionless hipster with a furrowed brow and a heavy heart, one could easily assume they were on the hunt for a café that served chai. Though in some areas of hipster hubs this hunt doesn't last long, there's nothing more heartbreaking than seeing a chai-less stray hipster.

Whisky — If a small bar devotes an entire wall to a range of whisky blends, then it obviously possesses a remedial understanding of alcohol. Besides, whisky is the only real drink you can pair with a hipster beard.

Artisanal Spirits — An easy way to know if a hipster digs artisanal spirits is if they're reading a copy of *Artisanal Spirits* magazine, or if their sleeve boasts cutesy, intricately detailed tattoos of brewing barrels.

Kombucha — The internet describes this beverage as "any of a variety of fermented, lightly effervescent sweetened black or green tea drinks that are commonly used as functional beverages for their unsubstantiated health benefits". But all of that is noise, as the sole reason hipsters dig the stuff is so they get to say 'Kombucha'.

Smith Street Books

Published in 2016 by Smith Street Books
Melbourne | Australia
smithstreetbooks.com

ISBN: 978 1 925418 03 3

CIP data is available from the National Library of Australia.

Publisher: Paul McNally
Design concept: Kate Barraclough
Design layout: Heather Menzies
Illustrator: Carla McRae
Editor: Hannah Koelmeyer

Printed & bound in China by C&C Offset Printing Co., Ltd.

Book 2
10 9 8 7 6 5 4 3 2